dabblelab

10-MINUTE
DUCT TAPE
PROJECTS

BY SARAH L. SCHUETTE

CAPSTONE PRESS
a capstone imprint

Dabble Lab is published by Capstone Press, an imprint of Capstone.
1710 Roe Crest Drive, North Mankato, Minnesota 56003
www.capstonepub.com

Library of Congress Cataloging-in-Publication Data is available on the Library of Congress website
ISBN 978-1-5435-9098-2 (library binding)
ISBN 978-1-5435-9104-0 (eBook PDF)

Summary: Need some fast and easy duct tape projects for your makerspace? You're in luck! From spinners and beads to wallets and bookmarks, these engaging 10-minute projects will have kids making in no time!

Editorial Credits
Editor: Shelly Lyons; Designer: Tracy McCabe;
Media Researcher: Tracy Cummins; Production Specialist: Katy LaVigne;
Project Production: Marcy Morin

Photo Credits
All photographs by Capstone: Karon Dubke

Design Elements
Shutterstock: Abra Cadabraaa, AllNikArt, BewWanchai, Bjoern Wylezich, casejustin, DarkPlatypus, Evgeniya Pautova, H Art, il67, keport, Maaike Boot, Maria Konstantinova, mila kad, Minur, Ninya Pavlova, olllikeballoon, Sooa, Tanya Sun, Tiwat K, Tukang Desain, Yes - Royalty Free

All internet sites appearing in back matter were available and accurate when this book was sent to press.

TABLE OF CONTENTS

GOT 1⏱ MINUTES?

Grab some supplies and get started! These quick and easy projects will inspire you. Simple supplies and easy directions will have you making in no time! And don't forget to clean up after yourself when you're done.

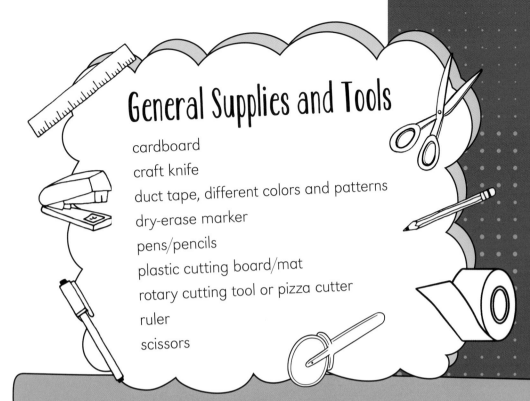

General Supplies and Tools

cardboard

craft knife

duct tape, different colors and patterns

dry-erase marker

pens/pencils

plastic cutting board/mat

rotary cutting tool or pizza cutter

ruler

scissors

Tips

- Gather the supplies and tools needed *before* starting a project.

- A rotary cutting tool is very sharp! Ask an adult to help you with sharp tools like this.

- Dry-erase markers work great for tracing or drawing on duct tape. Just wipe away the marks if you don't want them to show.

- When making a long project, cut shorter strips and tape them together. Long single strips of tape can be tough to handle.

- To make clean cuts, stick duct tape to a plastic mat. Use a rotary cutting tool to cut the strips. Peel the tape up from the board and add it to your project. If the piece of tape is too short, just stick on a new piece.

- Change things up! Don't be afraid to make these projects your own.

SQUISHY PAL

Have you ever wanted to create your own
stuffed animal? Now is your chance!
This squishy pal makes the perfect playmate.

What You Need:

5 duct tape strips, about
    10 inches (25 centimeters) long

cutting board

scissors

cotton balls, old socks,
    or anything squishy

additional duct tape

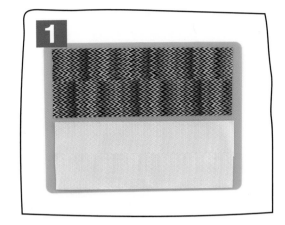

What You Do:

1 Stick one strip of duct tape to a cutting board. Add a second strip on top, overlapping the long edge by ¼ inch (0.64 cm). Repeat with two more strips of tape, but with sticky parts facing up. You will have two large tape rectangles.

2 Place one large rectangle on top of the other, sticky sides together.

3 Fold the rectangle in half widthwise to make a pouch.

4 Cut the remaining strip of duct tape in half widthwise. Use it to tape the sides of the pouch shut.

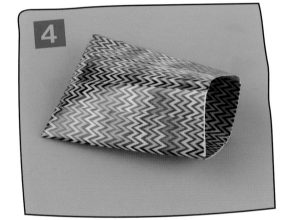

5 Stuff the pouch with cotton balls or old socks. Tape the top of the pouch shut.

6 Use more duct tape to add a horn, eyes, or any features you like.

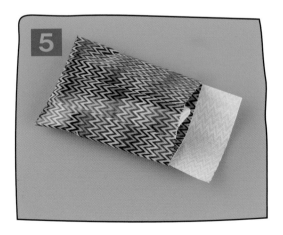

TIP Skip the stuffing and leave the pouch open. Add a duct tape strap to make a bag.

FEATHER BACKPACK PULL

Jazz up your backpack zipper with a cute feather. You can easily make this into earrings, a necklace, or a pin too.

What You Need:

1 duct tape strip, about 8 inches (20 cm) long

dry-erase marker

scissors or rotary cutting tool

awl (optional)

metal clasp or ring/paper clip

What You Do:

1 Fold the duct tape strip in half widthwise, sticky sides together.

2 Draw a feather or raindrop shape on the front of the tape with the dry-erase marker.

3 Cut out the shape. Then make small cuts along the edges to create fringe.

4 Poke a hole in the top of the feather with scissors or an awl.

5 Slide a metal clasp, ring, or paper clip through the hole. Attach to your backpack zipper.

TIP Try using a pizza cutter or any rotary cutting tool to make exact cuts in your duct tape creations.

BEAUTIFUL BEADS

Want to decorate your wrist? Twirl a bunch of duct tape beads and string them together to make a funky bracelet. Then show your friends your new jewelry!

What You Need:

4 duct tape strips, about ½ inch (1.3 cm) wide

scissors

paper straw

yarn or string, long enough to wrap around your wrist

additional duct tape in different colors

plastic beads, feathers, or charms (optional)

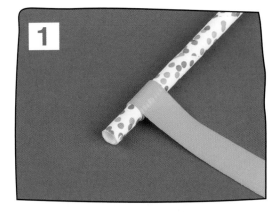

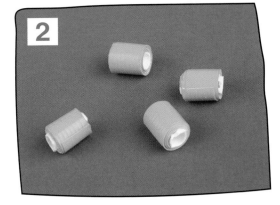

What You Do:

1 Stick each duct tape strip to a paper straw. Roll the straws to make bead shapes with the tape.

2 Cut the straw at each side of every bead. The straw shouldn't stick out past the ends of the tape beads.

3 Thread the yarn or string through the beads.

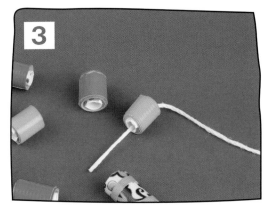

4 Repeat steps 1–2 to make more beads and build your bracelet. Change the size of the tape strips to make longer or thicker beads. Add thinner strips of tape on top of the beads to add a second color.

5 Tie a knot to end the bracelet.

TIP Team up with friends and make friendship bracelets for each other. Add in plastic beads, feathers, or charms!

11

GIANT LETTER TILE

Pick a letter and create a tile. Work together with friends to create a meaningful word to display at home or school.

What You Need:

1 cardboard square, about 8x8 inches (20x20 cm)

additional duct tape, 3 colors

ruler

cutting board

dry-erase marker

scissors

What You Do:

1 Wrap a cardboard square in one color of duct tape. Wrap the edges with a second color of tape.

2 Stick a 3½ inch (8.9 cm) piece of duct tape to a cutting board. Draw a letter on top with a dry-erase marker.

3 Cut out the letter and stick it to the middle of the square.

4 Work with friends to spell out a colorful word to display at school or home.

DESK STATION

Design your own desk station! Jot down important reminders, or show off your latest drawings in style. Plus, store all your stuff in these cute containers.

What You Need:

1 cardboard square, about 8x8 inches (20x20 cm)

scissors

dry-erase sheet or tape

cardboard box and cardboard tube

additional duct tape

dry-erase markers

What You Do:

1 Wrap the cardboard square in a sticky dry-erase sheet or tape.

2 Wrap a small cardboard box and cardboard tube in duct tape. Make sure to cover one end of the tube with tape.

3 Stick the box and tube to the cardboard square with more duct tape.

4 Use more duct tape to decorate the board. Be creative!

TIP This handy desk station can be turned into a locker station. Just stick it to your locker door with more duct tape!

PICTURE PROP

Do you like taking pictures and selfies?
Get goofy and create a silly prop for your pics!

What You Need:

1 duct tape strip, about 12 inches (25 cm) long

dry-erase marker

scissors or rotary cutting tool

additional duct tape

craft stick

digital camera or phone camera

What You Do:

1 Fold the duct tape strip in half widthwise, sticky sides together.

2 Draw a bow tie, glasses, or other fun shape on the duct tape with the marker.

3 Cut out the shape.

4 Tape the shape to a craft stick.

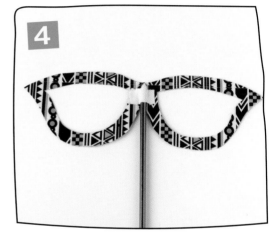

TIP Work together with friends to create a bunch of fun props. Make your own photo booth by hanging a colorful sheet on a wall or in a doorway. Then start snapping your goofy pics with those props!

PROP BOX
WITH BOW

Now that you have props for your photos, make a duct tape box to store them in. You'll smile every time you unpack the box. You can even make your own bow!

What You Need:

3 duct tape strips, about
8 inches (20 cm) long

additional duct tape

1 duct tape strip, about
4 inches (10 cm) long

cardboard box, about
16x13 inches (41x33 cm)

What You Do:

1 Fold all three 8-inch (20-cm) strips of duct tape in half lengthwise, sticky sides together.

2 Fold each strip so the ends meet in the middle. Tape the ends down.

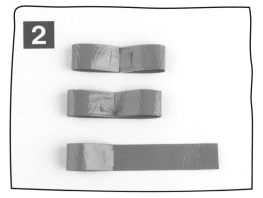

3 Set the pieces on top of each other and fan them out like a bow. Tape the strips where they meet in the middle.

4 Fold the 4-inch (10-cm) tape strip in half lengthwise, sticky sides together. Then fold it together as you did in Step 2. Tape it on top of the bow.

5 Decorate a cardboard box with duct tape and add the bow on top.

TIP This beautiful box can be used for gift-giving too!

19

MAGIC WALLET

Amaze your friends with this tricky wallet.
The money inside will magically change places!

What You Need:

- 2 pieces of cardboard, about 3x5 inches (7.6x13 cm)
- 2 duct tape strips, about 10 inches (25 cm) long
- additional duct tape
- scissors or rotary cutting tool

What You Do:

1 Cover both sides of each piece of cardboard with duct tape.

2 Fold each duct tape strip in half lengthwise. Cut each strip in half to make four pieces.

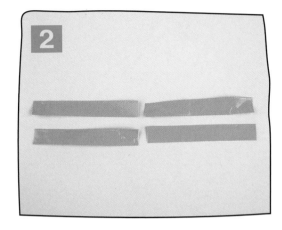

3 Use two strips to make an X in the center of one cardboard piece. Place a third strip above the X. Place the last strip below the X.

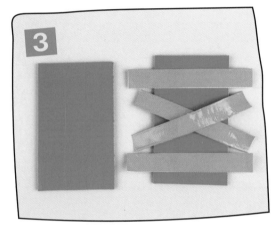

4 Set the second cardboard piece on top of the strips. On the left side, tape the ends of the top and bottom strips to the cardboard.

5 On the right side, tape the ends of the X to the cardboard.

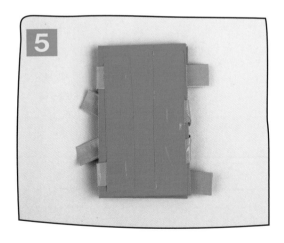

6 Flip over the whole thing. Then stick the remaining tape ends to the cardboard.

TIP Slide a dollar bill between the two parallel strips. Flip the wallet back and forth. You'll be amazed at how the money inside moves from side to side.

SPINNING TOP

Keep your hands busy with this simple
spinning top. Give your top a twirl
and see how long it spins!

What You Need:

pencil

duct tape

cardboard

scissors

1 wooden dowel, about
2½ inches (6.4 cm) long

bead with large hole

What You Do:

1 Trace the inside of a roll of duct tape onto cardboard. Cut out the circle and cover with duct tape.

2 Slide one end of the dowel into the hole in the bead. Wrap the other end of the dowel with tape.

3 Cut an X in the center of the cardboard circle. The X should be just big enough to hold the bead. Push the bead, with the stick pointing up, through the hole. The bead should poke out on each side of the circle.

4 Twist the stick and let it go. Watch the spinner spin!

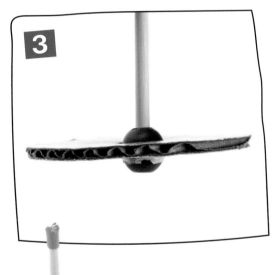

DECAL CRAZY!

Decorate your school supplies with duct tape. Make your pencils, notebooks, and bulletin boards unique with your own duct tape decals.

What You Need:

duct tape

wax paper or parchment paper

marker

scissors or rotary cutting tool

What You Do:

1 Stick duct tape to a piece of wax paper.

2 Flip the wax paper over. Then draw a shape where the duct tape is.

3 Cut out the shape. Then peel the wax paper off the shape.

4 Stick the decal wherever you'd like!

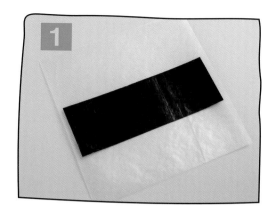

BOOKMARK

Mark your spot in style! This quick and easy
bookmark will make reading even more fun.

What You Need:

1 piece of card stock, 2x5 inches (5.1x13 cm)

1 duct tape strip, about 10 inches (25 cm) long

hole punch

ribbon

additional duct tape

What You Do:

1 Lay the piece of card stock over half of the sticky side of the piece of duct tape.

2 Fold the tape to cover the other side of the card stock.

3 Punch a hole in one end of the bookmark.

4 Tie a piece of ribbon through the hole.

5 Decorate the bookmark with smaller strips of duct tape.

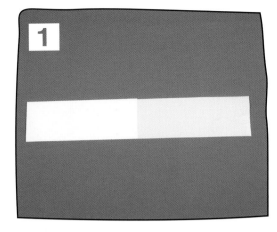

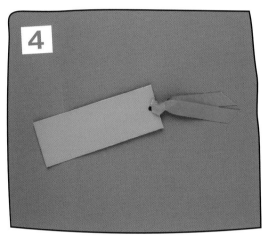

TABLET
HOLDER

Keep your tech gear safe and secure
with a tablet holder that's totally your style.

What You Need:

one piece of card stock, 8.5x11 inches (22x28 cm)

duct tape, different colors

2 duct tape strips, about 8 inches (20 cm) long

1 duct tape strip, about 4 inches (10 cm) long

hook-and-loop fasteners

What You Do:

1 Cover both sides of the card stock with duct tape.

2 Fold the covered card stock in half.

3 Stick one 8-inch (20-cm) strip of duct tape to a cutting board. Add the second strip, overlapping the long edge by ¼ inch (0.6 cm). Then fold it, sticky parts together. This piece will be a pocket.

4 Attach the pocket to the inside bottom corner of the holder with extra pieces of tape.

5 Fold the 4-inch (10-cm) strip in half, lengthwise. Tape half of the strip to the back cover.

6 Remove the backing from the fastener. Add one side of it to the sticky end of the tape strip. Stick the other part of the fastener to the front cover, where it will meet up with the first part.

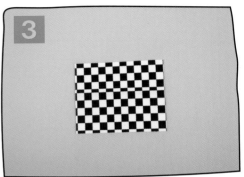

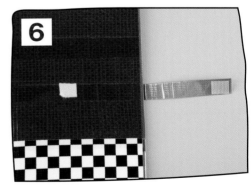

TIP Use the strap to keep the tablet holder closed when you aren't using it.

PENCIL TOPPER

Add some flair to your writing tool with a duct tape flower! Challenge yourself to make different sizes, shapes, and color combinations.

What You Need:

2 duct tape strips, about
   12 inches (30 cm) long

scissors

pencil

What You Do:

1 Lay one piece of duct tape sticky side up. Lay the other piece on top, sticky side down, leaving ¼ inch (0.6 cm) of the sticky part showing on each strip.

2 Fold the tape over to make a tube opening. Then stick it down on itself.

3 Cut small slits along the folded side of the tape tube. Do not cut all the way through.

4 Stick the tape, slit side out, to the eraser end of a pencil. Wrap the tape around the eraser to make a bow or flower. Use extra tape to secure it to the pencil.

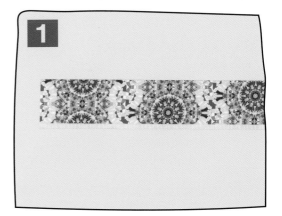

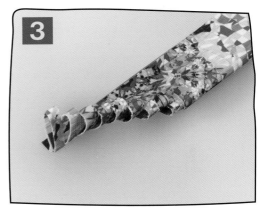

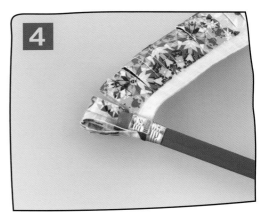

Read More

Bernhardt, Carolyn. *Duct Tape Fashion*. Minneapolis: Lerner, 2017 .

Felix, Rebecca. *Duct Tape Survival Gear.* Minneapolis: Lerner, 2017.

Petelinsek, Kathleen. *Crafting with Duct Tape: Even More Projects*. Ann Arbor, MI: Cherry Lake Publishing, 2016.

Ventura, Marne. *My First Guide to Duct Tape Projects*. North Mankato, MN: Capstone Press, 2017.

Internet Sites

Education.com: Duct Tape Bracelets
https://www.education.com/activity/article/duct-tape-bracelets/

Hip2Save: Duct Tape Pencil Pouches (Easy Back to School Craft)
https://hip2save.com/2014/08/05/duct-tape-pencil-pouches-easy-back-to-school-craft/

Sensibly Sara: Duct Tape Bookmarks: Easy-to-Make Craft
https://sensiblysara.com/duct-tape-bookmarks-craft/

The Spruce Crafts: 11 Fun and Easy Duct Tape Crafts
https://www.thesprucecrafts.com/duct-tape-crafts-1251006

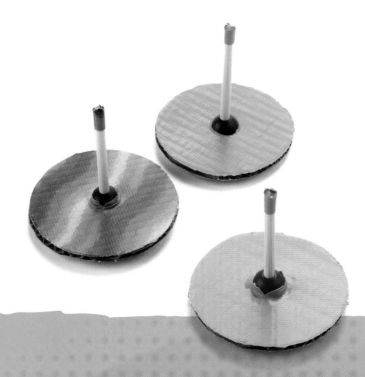